Tobias Picker
b.1954

Car Aria
from *An American Tragedy*
for Tenor and Piano

Libretto by Gene Scheer
Based on a story by Theodore Dreiser

ED 30043

www.schott-music.com

Mainz · London · Madrid · New York · Paris · Prague · Tokyo · Toronto
© 2010 SCHOTT HELICON MUSIC CORPORATION, New York · Printed in USA

TOBIAS PICKER

Car Aria

from *An American Tragedy*
for Tenor and Piano

Schott Helicon Music Corporation

ED 30043

Car Aria

from "An American Tragedy"

(version for Tenor)

Gene Scheer

Tobias Picker

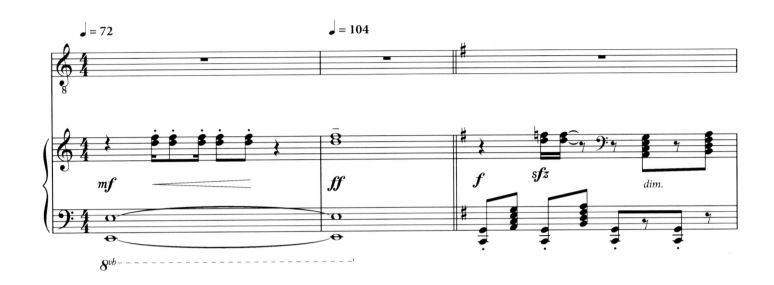

Hymns and prayers, hymns and prayers. Noth-ing___ but dis - dain - ful stares.___

But look at me now! Fif - teen a

week and run-ning___ this floor!___ Hard work___ and hope.___ A few years___ from now___

___ I can___ see it: more!___

That pret-ty girl.— What was her name? I be-lieve, I be-lieve, yes, Ro-ber-ta that's

Schott Helicon Music Corporation

254 West 31st Street, 15th Floor
New York, NY 10001
Tel: 212 461 6940
Fax: 212 810 4565
ny@schott-music.com

HL 49018268
ISBN: 978-1-61780-329-1

ISBN-13: 978-1-61780-329-1

Distributed By

HAL LEONARD

49018268   9 781617 803291

DISTRIBUTED IN NORTH AND SOUTH AMERICA
EXCLUSIVELY BY
HAL LEONARD
CORPORATION
49018268   8 84088 54726 4